Space Voyager

Saturn

by Vanessa Black

Bullfrog Books

Ideas for Parents and Teachers

Bullfrog Books let children practice reading informational text at the earliest reading levels. Repetition, familiar words, and photo labels support early readers.

Before Reading
- Discuss the cover photo. What does it tell them?
- Look at the picture glossary together. Read and discuss the words.

Read the Book
- "Walk" through the book and look at the photos. Let the child ask questions. Point out the photo labels.
- Read the book to the child, or have him or her read independently.

After Reading
- Prompt the child to think more. Ask: What are your favorite facts about Saturn?

Bullfrog Books are published by Jump!
5357 Penn Avenue South
Minneapolis, MN 55419
www.jumplibrary.com

Copyright © 2018 Jump! International copyright reserved in all countries. No part of this book may be reproduced in any form without written permission from the publisher.

Library of Congress Cataloging-in-Publication Data

Names: Black, Vanessa, 1973– author.
Title: Saturn / by Vanessa Black.
Description: Minneapolis, MN : Jump!, Inc., [2018]
Series: Space voyager
Audience: Age 5–8. | Audience: K to grade 3.
Includes index.
Identifiers: LCCN 2017028593 (print)
LCCN 2017033282 (ebook)
ISBN 9781624966903 (ebook)
ISBN 9781620318522 (hardcover : alk. paper)
ISBN 9781620318539 (pbk.)
Subjects: LCSH: Saturn (Planet) —Juvenile literature.
Classification: LCC QB671 (ebook)
LCC QB671 .B59 2018 (print) | DDC 523.46—dc23
LC record available at https://lccn.loc.gov/2017028593

Editor: Jenna Trnka
Book Designer: Molly Ballanger
Photo Researchers: Molly Ballanger & Jenna Trnka

Photo Credits: NASA images/Shutterstock, cover; Fuse/Getty, 1; Portland Press Herald/Getty, 3; MarcelClemens/Shutterstock, 4, 23bl; NASA/JPL-Caltech/Michael Benson/Getty, 5; Digital Vision/Getty, 6-7; dedek/Shutterstock, 8–9, 23tr; Science Photo Library - Mark Garlick/Getty, 10–11, 23tl; Sightseeing Archive/Getty, 12; Tristan3D/Shutterstock, 13; JPL-Caltech/Space Science Institute/NASA, 14–15; SPL/Science Source, 16; NASA/Getty, 17; David Ducros/Science Source, 18–19, 23br; inhauscreative/iStock, 20–21; adventtr/iStock, 23tr; JPL/NASA, 24.

Printed in the United States of America at Corporate Graphics in North Mankato, Minnesota.

Table of Contents

A Lot of Rings

Saturn is a planet.

It is in our solar system.

rings

It has many rings!

What are they?

Pieces of ice and rock.

Look!

Some are big.

Some are small.

Saturn is the sixth
planet from the sun.

It does not get
much sunlight.

Brr!

It is cold.

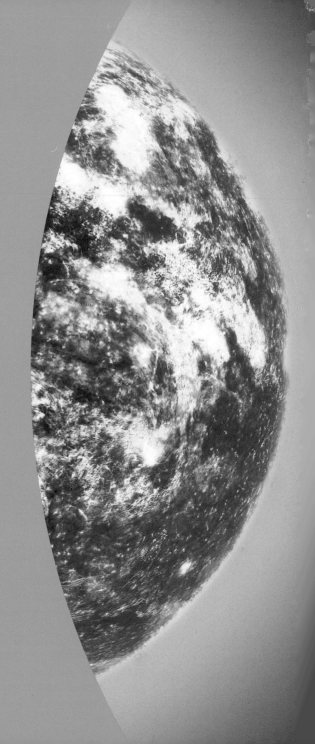

It orbits the sun.

It is slow.

One year there is
29 Earth years!

Saturn is big.

It is the second biggest planet.

Only Jupiter is bigger.

Jupiter ·····▶

13

It is almost all gas.

You would not be
able to stand on it.

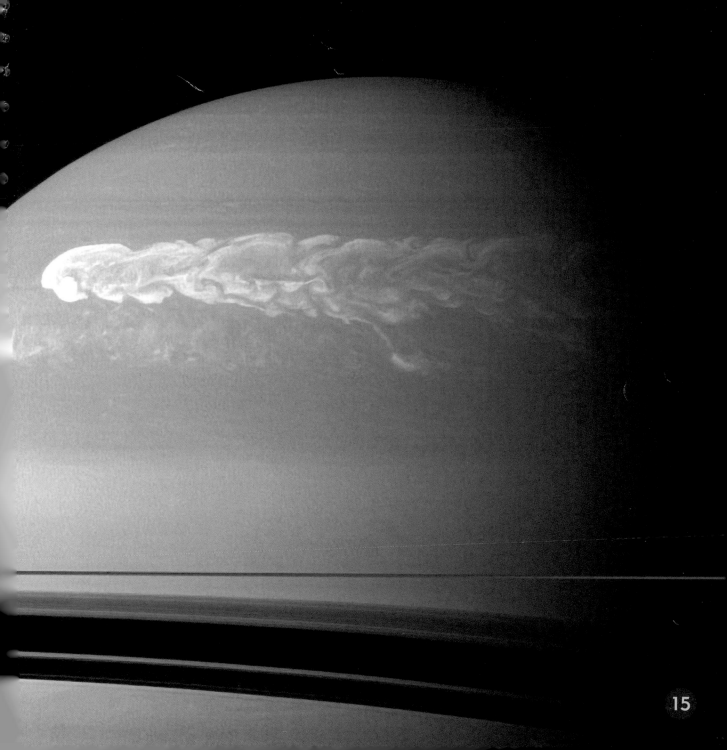

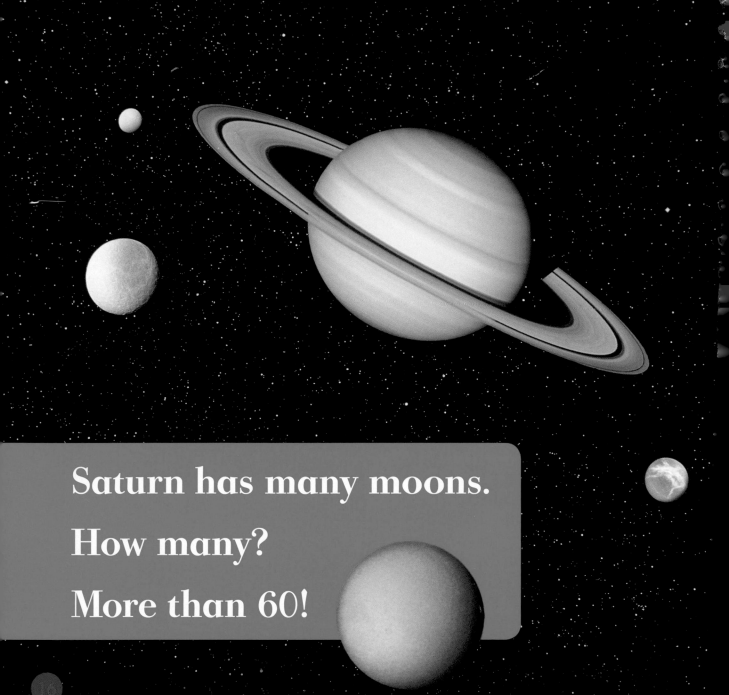

Saturn has many moons.
How many?
More than 60!

The biggest is Titan.

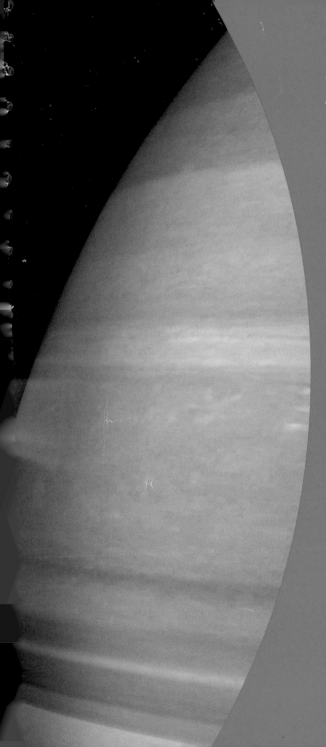

How do we know?

Spacecraft.

They take photos.

Wow!

Why do you like Saturn?

A Look at Saturn

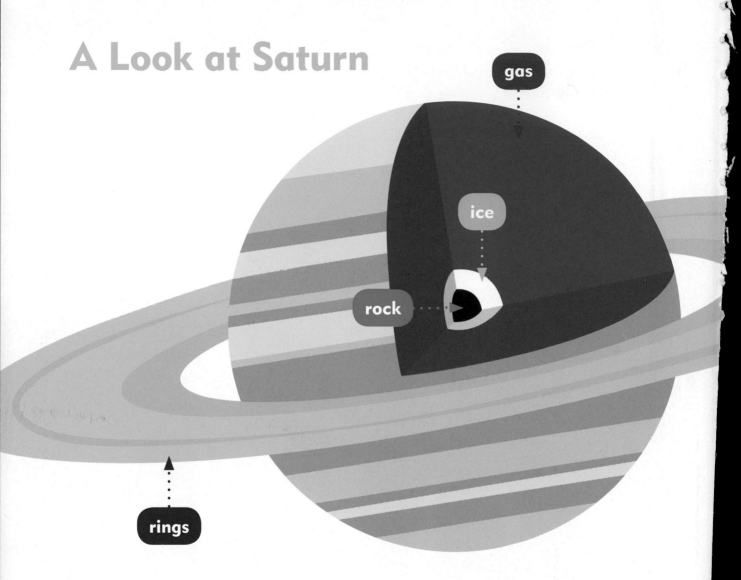

gas

ice

rock

rings

Picture Glossary

orbits
Travels around
in circles.

solar system
The sun and
other planets that
revolve around it.

planet
A large body that
orbits the sun.

spacecraft
Vehicles that
travel in space.

Index

To Learn More

Learning more is as easy as 1, 2, 3.

1) Go to www.factsurfer.com

2) Enter "Saturn" into the search box.

3) Click the "Surf" button to see a list of websites.

With factsurfer.com, finding more information is just a click away.